Skills Map

What is critical thinking?
Familiarise yourself with the basics of evaluation and practise distinguishing between fact and opinion.

Recognising strong or sound arguments
Learn how to construct strong or sound arguments and how to better recognise these in the work of others.

Recognising poor arguments
Learn how to recognise faulty reasoning in the arguments of others.

Persuasion through language or pressure
Explore the manipulation of argumentation by the use of a variety of linguistic techniques.

Detecting bias
Consider important questions about authors' selection and presentation of materials.

Putting it into practice
Put into practice the skills you have learnt in this module by preparing for and taking part in a seminar.

Destination: Critical Thinking

What is critical thinking?

At the end of this unit you will be able to:
- understand the difference between thinking and critical thinking;
- recognise the difference between a fact and an opinion;
- use a framework to evaluate arguments.

Task 1 Thinking skills

1.1 Working alone, find the 'odd one out'.

For example:

aba aba aba aba aba (bba) aba aba

a) ✓ ✓ ✓ ✓ ✗ ✓ ✓ ✓ ✓ ✓ ✓

b) ♠ ♥ ♠ ♠ ♠ ♠ ♠ ♠ ♠

c) ‖ ‖ ‖ ‖ ‖ ‖ ‖ ‖ L ‖ ‖ ‖ ‖ ‖

d) ttf tft tft tft tft tft tft tft tft tft

1.2 Working alone, fill in the next item in the sequences below.

For example:

✓ ✗ ✓ ✗ ✓ ✗ ✓ ... = ✗

a) ■ ▲ ◆ ● ■ ...

b) ✓ ✓ ✓ ✗ ✓ ✓ ...

c) 1 2 3 5 8 13 ...

d) 2 4 8 16 32 ...

1.3 Now work with a partner and compare your answers. Then discuss what steps you took to find the answers.

Task 2 Critical thinking skills

To answer the two exercises in Task 1, you compared items in a sequence and looked for patterns. These are two examples of thinking skills which you probably use every day, maybe to predict if your bus is likely to be next or to put your clothes away in the right places (socks in a drawer, shirts in a wardrobe, etc.). Critical thinking is based on these everyday thinking skills which you use all the time.

Generally, critical thinking is used to understand and evaluate arguments. It is not important whether you agree or disagree with the arguments. Rather, critical thinking requires you to recognise that an argument is a good one, even if you disagree with it, or that another is a bad one, even if you agree with its conclusions.

2.1 Read the following argument carefully.

> English has become a global language for a number of reasons. From an historical perspective, it spread to many parts of the world when successive waves of English speakers migrated abroad from the UK. In terms of the language itself, it is relatively easy to learn with its vocabulary, which is borrowed from many different languages, and its fairly simple grammar. The economic dominance of English-speaking countries for many centuries has also contributed to its status as a global language. Indeed, English is likely to remain the number one global language for ever.

2.2 Discuss the following questions with your partner.

a) What does the writer of this argument want you to believe?

b) How does the writer try to persuade you?

c) What is the writer's conclusion?

d) Is the writer's argument logical? Why/Why not?

Task 3 Facts or opinions?

" It's got a powerful engine. "

" It's too fast to drive on public roads. "

Unit 1

In academic work, it is important to distinguish a fact from an opinion. A fact is a piece of information which can be checked and proved. Something is a fact if, for example, we can observe it, test it or check it against some evidence. In contrast, an opinion is something which someone thinks is true. Unlike a fact, an opinion cannot be proved. However, sometimes the distinction between a fact and an opinion is not clear to us because so many people share the same opinion. Equally, new evidence may disprove something which was once considered a fact.

3.1 Look at the following statements. Which one is a fact and which one is an opinion? When you have finished, compare your ideas with your partner.

> English is a very easy language to learn.

> English is spoken all over the world.

3.2 Now look at the following statements about English. Underline opinions like this and facts like this.

For example:
English is better than other languages because it has a bigger vocabulary than other languages.

a) English has borrowed many words from a wide range of other languages. Examples include tycoon from Japanese, verandah from Hindi, gong from Javanese, slim from Dutch and junta from Spanish.

tycoon

verandah

gong
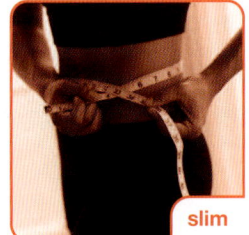
slim

junta

b) English is spoken in more countries than any other language.

c) English contains vocabulary which is borrowed from many other languages, and this is why it is a global language.

3.3 Work with a partner. Choose one of the essay titles below and make a note of any opinions which are directly stated in it or which indirectly support it.

a) Decisions about the practice of cloning should be made by experts who understand the science which is involved, not by the general public. Discuss.

b) Outline the main measures for the prevention of cancer.

c) A knowledge of Economics is essential for historians. Discuss.

d) One of the causes of juvenile delinquency is a result of poor attachment from birth. What might other causes be?

Task 4 Questioning opinions

In small groups, discuss what questions you would need to ask in order to accept, reject or suspend judgement of the opinions you have identified in one of the titles in Tasks 3.2 and 3.3. Write as many questions as you can think of.

For example:
Opinion: English is better than other languages.
Questions: Is English better than other languages?
In what ways is it 'better'?

Opinion:
Questions:

Opinion:
Questions:

Opinion:
Questions:

Opinion:
Questions:

Task 5 A checklist for evaluating research

The following five questions should be asked when critically evaluating others' or your own work. Some words have been removed. Use the words in the box below to complete the questions.

| evidence | unbiased | viewpoints | concepts | reasoning |

a) Is the issue under discussion clearly stated in a/n _____ fashion?

b) Is relevant _____, experience and/or information provided?

c) Are key _____ defined as necessary?

d) Is there a clear line of _____ arriving at logical conclusions?

e) Are alternate _____ presented?

Task 6 Putting evaluation into practice

6.1 Look at the following essay question and, working with a partner, underline the opinion.

The artificial language Esperanto would be a more appropriate global language than English in the twenty-first century. Discuss.

6.2 With your partner, discuss what questions you would need to ask in order to accept, reject or suspend judgement of the opinions you have identified.

6.3 Use the checklist in Task 5 to evaluate the essay below. Make notes and then compare your ideas with your partner's.

The artificial language Esperanto would be a more appropriate global language than English in the twenty-first century. Discuss.

Esperanto, which remains one of the best-loved artificial languages to date, was invented by the brilliant Ludwig Lazarus Zamenhof in the late nineteenth century. Zamenhof, a multilingual who spoke Russian, Yiddish, Polish, Hebrew, Latin, Greek, French, German and English, set out to develop an easy-to-learn universal second language which could help bring about world peace (Crystal, 1987).

How can a language help to bring about world peace? When he constructed Esperanto, Zamenhof hoped it would become a universal second language. He based his new language on a number of Indo-European languages. Its sounds are from Slavic, its vocabulary comes from a mixture of languages, including Latin, French, Spanish and German (Wells, 1989). As a result, it is not associated with any one nationality and may be considered a truly international language.

Due to its international status, Esperanto is now widely spoken around the world. Although estimates vary widely, it is thought to have between 100,000 and 15,000,000 speakers. By the 1970s, over 60 countries had a national Esperanto association (Crystal, 1987). It is thus a global language.

Given that it is so easy to learn, Esperanto could rapidly overtake English as the global language of the twenty-first century. For example, in the mid-1960s approximately 1,000,000 people in 74 countries signed a petition addressed to the United Nations in favour of Esperanto becoming an official international language (Auld, 1988). Although the United Nations eventually rejected this proposal, the petition is evidence of Esperanto's popularity.

In conclusion, Esperanto would clearly make a better global language than English in the future, as it does not belong to any one group of people and so its speakers are all equal. Moreover, Esperanto is a popular language, with speakers all over the world. This fact also makes it a better global language than English. Finally, Esperanto is a relatively new language compared with English. Arguably, Esperanto is the language of the future; English is the language of the past.

Bibliography

Auld E.F. Esperanto: the early struggle for recognition. Smiths Press, London 1988

6.4 We use critical thinking skills not only to evaluate other people's arguments, but also to improve our own. Use the checklist in Task 5 to evaluate a piece of your own writing. Make notes and then discuss your ideas with your partner.

Reflect

Consider the general thinking skills you use when you make everyday decisions: what to wear in the morning, what to eat for lunch, how to make use of your spare time. Choose a decision you have made today and try to analyse the process you went through to arrive at the decision. Reflect in the same way on other decisions you have made.

Compare these thinking skills with the critical thinking skills you have discussed in Unit 1. To what extent do you use them already to evaluate opinions and express your own opinions?

Think about your experience of people you know who have graduated from higher education studies. Bearing in mind what you have learnt in this unit, do you feel they use critical thinking skills to a greater extent than others?

Student notes for Unit 1

Unit 2 Recognising strong or sound arguments

At the end of this unit you will be able to:
- identify parts of arguments;
- understand the relationship between the parts of an argument.

In your university assessments, you will be rewarded for recognising and using strong and sound arguments. It is therefore important to understand what these are and to be able to build your own strong and sound arguments.

An argument can be divided into two parts: premises and a conclusion. Premises give evidence to support the conclusion. In some cases, the conclusion may not be directly stated, but it can be understood by the reader.

Task 1 Constructing an argument

1.1 Underline the *premises* and the *conclusion* in the following argument.
For example:

My tutor is always on time for her lessons, but today she is ten minutes late, so *something must have happened to her*!

Global warming is definitely happening. I don't care what people say, but it was hotter this year than it has ever been.

1.2 What are the unspoken premises in the following?

a) You can't travel to Bhutan without a visa, so Ali is going to have problems if he intends to fly out there tomorrow.

b) I heard on the radio this morning that Western Region trains will be very disrupted tomorrow, so Natalia will be late for the interview.

1.3 What are the unspoken conclusions in the following?

a) The student candidate who best reflects mainstream opinion is very likely to win the next student election. The policies put forward by Sarah Rollings most closely match popular opinion.

b) The ban on smoking in public places will hit profits in cafes and bars. My cousin owns a large chain of bars.

Task 2 Recognising sound or strong arguments

There are various types of arguments: valid, sound and strong.

2.1 **The following are examples of the three types of argument. Look at the three examples and underline the premises and the conclusions you find in them.**

a) Some manufactured food products contain nuts. Harry is severely allergic to nuts. Therefore, he should avoid certain manufactured foods.

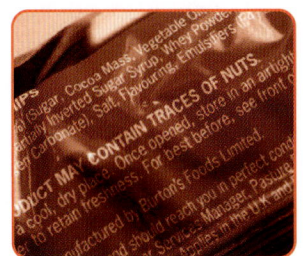

b) My aunt has sent me a cheque every year since I was five years old. Therefore, I expect to receive a cheque for my birthday this year too.

c) All Chinese people are good cooks. Ting Ting is Chinese so, as a consequence, she must be a good cook.

2.2 **Now read the definitions of the three types of argument. Match an example to each one. When you have finished, check with your partner.**

A valid argument
This is an argument where the conclusion absolutely follows from the premises, but the premises may not be true. ____

A sound argument
This is an argument where the conclusion absolutely follows from true premises. A sound argument is deductive (working from general to particular). ____

A strong argument
This is an argument where the conclusion does not necessarily follow from the premises, but if the premises are strong enough, the conclusion is likely to be true. A strong argument is inductive (working from particular to general). ____

A good argument should ideally be both sound and strong.

Task 3 Checking your understanding

3.1 Are the following statements true or false?

   a) Valid arguments are always good arguments.

   b) If a strong argument has a false conclusion, then not all its premises can be true.

   c) A sound argument can't have a false conclusion.

3.2 Match the type of argument and the example.

   a) A sound argument

   b) A valid argument

   c) A strong argument

   i) All dogs are black. Bingo is a dog, so Bingo must be black.

   ii) The food in this restaurant is always good, so we'll have a good meal today.

   iii) Brighton has a train station, so we can catch trains from Brighton.

3.3 Look at some arguments put forward in a seminar comparing the advantages and disadvantages of Esperanto and English as international languages. Decide if the arguments are valid, sound or strong. When you have finished, compare your answers with your partner's.

a An artificial language is far better than a natural one, so Esperanto is clearly superior to English.

b The number of Esperanto speakers has been increasing since the language's introduction in 1887, so next year there will be even greater numbers of Esperanto speakers in all probability.

c There are vastly more speakers of English than Esperanto, so when addressing someone who doesn't speak your language, using English is more likely to be successful than using Esperanto.

d Everybody speaks English already and only a few people speak Esperanto, so it makes more sense to use English, rather than Esperanto, as an international language.

e The vocabulary of Esperanto is largely borrowed from Western European languages. Consequently, Western Europeans have an advantage when learning its

f Outside Europe, large and active communities of Esperanto speakers can be found in China, Korea and Japan. If Esperanto continues to spread in Asia, it may rival English as an international language there in the future.

Task 4 Your examples

4.1 Write two examples of a sound argument based on your field of study.

4.2 Write two examples of a valid argument based on your field of study.

4.3 Write two examples of a strong argument based on your field of study.

4.4 Work with a partner and share your examples. Together, you have four examples of each type of argument (sound, valid and strong). Evaluate all four examples for each type and choose the best one. Then copy out your three examples onto a sheet of paper without saying which type of argument they exemplify. Swap papers with another pair. Match each example with a type of argument (sound, valid and strong). It may help to underline premises and conclusions to do this.

Reflect

Think about how your attitude to argumentation has changed now you have completed this unit. Reflect on discussions you have had in the past. Do you feel they generally used sound arguments?

Reflect on whether the way you discuss issues varies according to the situation you are in and the people you are with. Compare a late-night discussion with friends in a cafe or bar with a discussion with fellow students following a lecture.

Bearing in mind your thoughts on the above, do you feel it is always appropriate to use academic arguments in daily life?

Student notes for Unit 2

Unit 3 Recognising poor arguments

At the end of this unit you will be able to:
- recognise weak arguments;
- point out weak arguments politely.

In Unit 2, the focus was on recognising and building strong and sound arguments. Unit 3 turns to the topic of poor or weak argumentation. In academic work, it is important to recognise poor argumentation in other people's work so that you are able to criticise the writers' ideas, and in your own work so that you can improve it.

Task 1 Spotting fallacious arguments

1.1 Arguments where the conclusion does not naturally follow from the premises or is not likely to occur are called fallacies or are fallacious. Look at the example below and underline the premises and the conclusion.

" *Pita speaks Spanish, so he must have come from Spain originally.* "

1.2 Look at the arguments below. Underline their premises and their conclusions. Then discuss with your partner what is wrong with them as arguments?

a) He hasn't replied, so he can't have received my letter.

b) He does not wear glasses, so he must have excellent eyesight.

c) English is superior to other languages and, as a result, is a global language.

d) I've double-checked my essay, so there can't be any mistakes in it.

Task 2 Poor argumentation strategies

There are certain strategies which can be used in place of proper argumentation. The following exercise examines four of the most common.

2.1 Match the four strategies below with their explanations.

Strategies	Explanations
a) Being subjective.	1 This is where the speaker plays on your desire to conform and be the same as other people, but does not offer any premises or reasons why you should conform.
b) Appealing to common beliefs.	2 This is where the speaker tries to convince you of the validity of their opinion by making you annoyed rather than providing real evidence.
c) Invoking peer pressure.	3 This is where the speaker does not examine the claim critically. Instead, they refer to their own experience. This is an attempt to stop any further discussion.
d) Attempting to make others annoyed.	4 This is where the speaker uses the fact that many people believe something to be true as a reason for you to accept their argument.

2.2 Now match an example below to one of the four strategies. When you have finished, compare with a partner.

Examples

a) ____ Our taxes are so high and the government is planning to use the extra revenue raised for opening multicultural centres. This is a complete waste of taxpayers' money.

GOVERNMENT TO WASTE MORE TAXPAYERS' MONEY

b) ____ Everyone knows that living a rural life is preferable to the stresses of urban living.

URBAN LIVING CAUSES STRESS!

c) _____ The idea that we all need to eat five pieces of fruit or vegetables a day to be healthy may be true for some people, but it is definitely not true in my case.

FRUIT 'N VEG BAD FOR YOU!

d) _____ Harry Potter novels are childish and unsuitable for adults, so you should not read them.

HARRY DRIVES ADULTS POTTY!

2.3 How could each of the arguments above be made into a strong or sound argument? Work individually and then compare your ideas with your partner's.

Task 3 Checking your understanding

3.1 Read the excerpts from a seminar on the advantages and disadvantages of English and Esperanto as international languages. Label examples of poor argument strategies as:

   a) being subjective
   b) appealing to common beliefs
   c) invoking peer pressure
   d) attempting to make others angry

1   People who think that Esperanto is better than English are a bit strange.

2   Listen, I know what I'm talking about. I've been an Esperanto speaker for years, and I can tell you it is far easier to learn than English. It's a fact. End of discussion.

3   I'm sure the CIA has been involved in making English the international language. It's America's way of dominating the world. Doesn't it make your blood boil?

4   Nobody thinks that Esperanto will ever rival English as an international language.

3.2 **In seminars, it is important to point out when someone is using poor argumentation. We often do this by using a negative question form and softening language, e.g., *a bit* + negative idea adjective. Write a reply to the poor arguments given in Task 3.1, using softening language.**

" Aren't you exaggerating a little? "

" Haven't you got that slightly wrong? "

Your argument is subjective.

Isn't that argument a bit subjective?

1
2
3
4

Reflect

Consider what you have learnt about poor argumentation. Try to notice examples of poor argumentation over the next few days. Listen to informal and class discussions, and the arguments used in radio and TV debates.

Student notes for Unit 3

Unit 4 Persuasion through language or pressure

At the end of this unit you will be able to:
- recognise when language, rather than reason, is used to persuade;
- recognise when pressure, rather than reason, is used to persuade.

In English-speaking cultures, argument often occurs in contexts where there is opposition, for example in Parliament or in the law courts. In these places, an issue is explored through two or more people taking opposing viewpoints and 'attacking' each other's arguments. In this sense, the discussion is like a 'fight' or a 'duel'. However, there are (unspoken) rules about what is acceptable, just like in a duel.

Words are very powerful. We need to be aware of how others may use words, as their words are like 'weapons' in an argument. These language weapons may be used to manipulate us unfairly. Ideally, however, we should be persuaded by logical reasoning.

Task 1 Making an idea sound better or worse

Euphemisms are used when we want to make an idea that might have negative connotations more neutral or positive.

Euphemisms can be used in situations when we feel the need to be sensitive to others' feelings. For example, when we are talking to a friend whose father has died recently, we may prefer to say, 'I'm sorry to hear about your loss', rather than, 'I'm sorry to hear that your father has died'.

When we are talking about people fighting against a government, we can show our viewpoint by describing them as either *terrorists* or *freedom fighters*. When we choose one of these descriptions, we are painting the fighters in a bad light (terrorists) or a good light (freedom fighters). This choice of language may affect the listeners' viewpoint without them realising.

Freedom fighter or terrorist?

1.1 **Work in a group of 3–4 students. Discuss the following questions.**

a) Do euphemisms exist in your language?
b) Does your language have an expression like 'freedom fighter'?
c) In what sort of contexts do people use euphemisms?
d) Why do people use euphemisms?
e) Why should you avoid using euphemisms in academic argument?

Dysphemisms are used when we want to make a word more negative.

The word *terrorist* has a negative meaning, while the expression *freedom fighter* has a positive one, as we saw above. *Terrorist* is used by a person who is strongly critical of the soldier. In contrast, *freedom fighter* is used by someone who strongly approves of the soldier. Thus, the different choice of vocabulary indicates the speakers' different attitudes to the soldier.

Unit 4

1.2 Divide the following words into two lists according to whether they are euphemisms or dysphemisms. (They are all words and expressions that describe a person's appearance.) When you have finished, compare your answers with your partner's.

> skinny   slim   willow-like   bony   svelte   skeletal   fine-boned   scrawny

Euphemisms:
The speaker approves

Dysphemisms:
The speaker disapproves

1.3 What is the best way to find out if a word indicates a neutral, approving or disapproving attitude on the part of the speaker? Discuss with your partner.

1.4 Working with your partner, give a euphemism or dysphemism for the following:

(i) a toilet

(ii) to kill someone or something

(iii) being overweight

Task 2 Making something sound less important or serious

No! I'm fine! Just a few scratches.

When we downplay something, we try to make it seem less important or significant in order to further our own ends.

2.1 Add each word or punctuation mark in brackets to its sentence. Pay attention to its correct position in the sentence.

a) He is a teacher. (just)

b) It costs £20 a month to insure your life. (a mere)

c) She got her degree from a university in the Midlands. (' ')

2.2 Working with a partner, discuss what each of the rewritten sentences means.

Task 3 Making something seem more important or serious

Hyperbole is a huge overstatement which may be used to persuade people of our viewpoint. The strength of the overstatement may persuade us to believe what someone has said, even though they may not have given us any premises.

For example:

Mick Jagger is the most inventive musician who has ever lived.

The use of hyperbole in the above is designed to leave the reader thinking Mick Jagger must be a very good musician, even if he is not the most inventive musician who has ever lived.

3.1 Discuss the hyperbole in the following statements in groups of 3–4 and speculate why the speaker has used it.

a) 'I can't come to work because I have a serious illness. I have a headache.'

b) 'My parents won't let me stay out later than midnight. They're such fascists.'

c) 'It's the most boring film in the world!'

3.2 Working individually, write two more examples of hyperbole. Then read your examples to your group, and see if the other group members can decide why each piece of hyperbole might be used.

Unit 4 - Persuasion through language or pressure - Task: Critical thinking

Task 4 Pressuring the audience

Speakers and writers can push their audiences to agree by using pressure. They can suggest that:

a) <u>all people</u> would find their arguments logical and reasonable;

b) all people <u>who are like the listener/reader</u> would find their arguments logical and reasonable.

4.1 Read through the following statements and decide which category described above (a or b) they belong to. After you have finished, compare answers with your partner.

> " Anyone with half a brain understands that a natural language is better than an artificial one. "

> " It is clearly the case that Esperanto is easier to learn than English. "

> " Any educated person understands the value of English. "

> " Anyone can see that Esperanto could be learnt in weeks. "

> " As is universally acknowledged, English will always be the best global language. "

> " All intelligent people naturally recognise Esperanto's superiority over English. "

Task 5 Checking your understanding

5.1 Read the following transcript of a discussion between two students about Esperanto and English. Underline the words and phrases they use to try to influence their listener unfairly.

A: Anyone with half a brain can see that Esperanto is an easier language to learn than English. It doesn't have any irregular verbs ... and it has the smallest vocabulary ever of any language.

B: But the 'language' [the speaker makes a gesture with both hands] of Esperanto is totally unknown. Who speaks it? No one.

A: Unknown! It has one or two fewer speakers than English, but the difference in numbers is minimal.

B: You're joking! Esperanto has a handful of speakers and there's a reason for that. It's OK for chitchat, but you can't have a serious conversation in it.

A: Well, we're speaking English now and I wouldn't call this a serious conversation!

5.2 Compare your answers with your partner's. Discuss what happens to a discussion when language is used to persuade unfairly.

Reflect

In this unit, we have studied the use of indirect language by English speakers. Think about the problems that this style of communication causes speakers from cultures which prefer direct expression.

Can you remember any situations where someone has used euphemisms, dysphemisms, hyperbole or pressure in an argument? How did you respond?

Student notes for Unit 4

Unit 5 — Detecting bias

At the end of this unit you will be able to:
- consider sources of bias in evidence in academic research;
- identify possible reasons for researcher bias.

A critical thinker must ask him or herself questions about who has written a text or which body might be funding the research in order to decide whether or not the text may have been affected by things such as personal agendas or vested interests.

Task 1 Detecting possible bias – Interviews

In some academic disciplines, interviews are used to collect evidence. These interviews can provide detailed information which is difficult to obtain from other sources. However, the information given by the interviewee may not be accurate.

1.1 Working in a small group, brainstorm reasons why interviewees may not give a totally accurate picture. Write the list of possible reasons in the space below.

1.2 Discuss the following questions with your group. During your discussion, think about the following.

- the content of the questions
- choice of vocabulary and language style
- question types *Wh-* or *Yes/No* questions
- differences in age, gender or culture

a) An interview is an interaction between two or more people. How might the interviewer affect what the interviewee says?

b) What can the interviewer do to minimise his or her impact on the interviewee?

Task 2 Detecting possible bias – Researchers and sources of funding

The relationship between a researcher and the research or the source of funding for the research might also affect the findings.

2.1 **Working in a small group, discuss what *possible* bias might be involved in the following situations.**

   a) A research report on nicotine and tobacco sponsored by the Tobacco Manufacturers' Association.
   b) A study on student library use conducted by a library threatened with closure.
   c) An ethnography of migrants living in Birmingham written by a British person.
   d) A research report sponsored by a cereal manufacturer on the impact of fibre on a diet.
   e) Analysis of a questionnaire on student satisfaction with a course carried out by the course director.

2.2 **Working with a partner, discuss the following questions.**

   a) What could the researchers involved in the projects described above do in order to deal with the problem of possible bias?
   b) What could a student do to find out whether a writer or source of information might be biased?

Task 3 Avoiding bias

Researchers are starting to reflect more on who they are and how their identity affects their beliefs and actions. They then share this information with their audience. This is known as reflexivity. Reflexivity has two benefits: it allows the reader to assess the work in question more easily and it reduces the possibility of the writer being criticised for being biased.

3.1 **Imagine you are going to write a report on how successful non-native students are at British universities. If you included this type of description of yourself in your report, which of the following elements might it be useful for your reader to know?**

   a) Your age
   b) Your religion
   c) Your star sign
   d) Your political affiliation
   e) Your nationality
   f) Your weight
   g) Your marital status
   h) Your gender
   i) Your sponsorship (if any)

j) Your hobbies

k) Your class

l) Your educational background

m) ....

n) ....

o) ....

3.2 Discuss with your partner any further elements to add to the list and write your ideas above.

3.3 Using the elements you selected, write a brief description of yourself which outlines how your personal identity impacts on your practice.

Reflect

In this unit, we have studied the problem of bias. Think about your own area of study. Is it possible to be entirely objective?

You will need to convince others of your objectivity both during your studies and after you graduate. How do you think you will do this?

Student notes for Unit 5

Unit 6 Putting it into practice

At the end of this unit you will be able to:
- use your critical thinking skills to construct your own arguments;
- evaluate your own and others' arguments using your critical thinking skills;
- recognise different styles of arguing;
- put together the skills you have developed in the earlier parts of the module.

The outcome of this unit will be a discussion of the following question: can local cultures be preserved despite the globalisation of culture?

Task 1 Understanding the question

1.1 **In small groups, discuss the following questions, keeping notes of your discussion.**

   a) How can you define 'culture'?

   b) What do you understand by the phrase 'globalisation of culture'?

   c) What examples can you give of 'local cultures'?

   d) What does the word 'preserve' mean?

   e) What attitude towards culture does the word 'preserve' suggest?

   f) What does the word 'can' mean in the context of this essay title?

1.2 **Working in pairs, write a list of statements which the discussion question presents as facts. Then compare your list with another pair's list and discuss whether, in your opinion, the statements are facts or not.**

1.3 Working individually, try to rewrite the following statement in your own words. You can use more than one sentence if you wish.

Local cultures can be preserved despite the globalisation of culture.

Task 2 Your view

It is important to be clear about your views on the discussion question.

2.1 Working individually, read the following statements and put a cross on each line to show how far you agree or disagree with the statements.

Culture is becoming globalised.

| 1 | 2 | 3 | 4 | 5 | 6 | 7 | 8 | 9 | 10 |

Completely agree — Completely disagree

Local cultures are valuable.

| 1 | 2 | 3 | 4 | 5 | 6 | 7 | 8 | 9 | 10 |

Completely agree — Completely disagree

It is possible to preserve local cultures.

| 1 | 2 | 3 | 4 | 5 | 6 | 7 | 8 | 9 | 10 |

Completely agree — Completely disagree

It is desirable to preserve local cultures.

| 1 | 2 | 3 | 4 | 5 | 6 | 7 | 8 | 9 | 10 |

Completely agree — Completely disagree

2.2 Compare your opinions with those of your partner. Give reasons for your opinions.

2.3 Work in a small group and discuss the following questions.

a) What are the alternatives to preserving local cultures?

b) What would the consequences of these alternatives be in your opinion?

c) Would these consequences be desirable? For whom?

Task 3 Gathering information

3.1 Working in a small group, discuss what questions you need to research in order to discuss this topic. Add them to the list below.

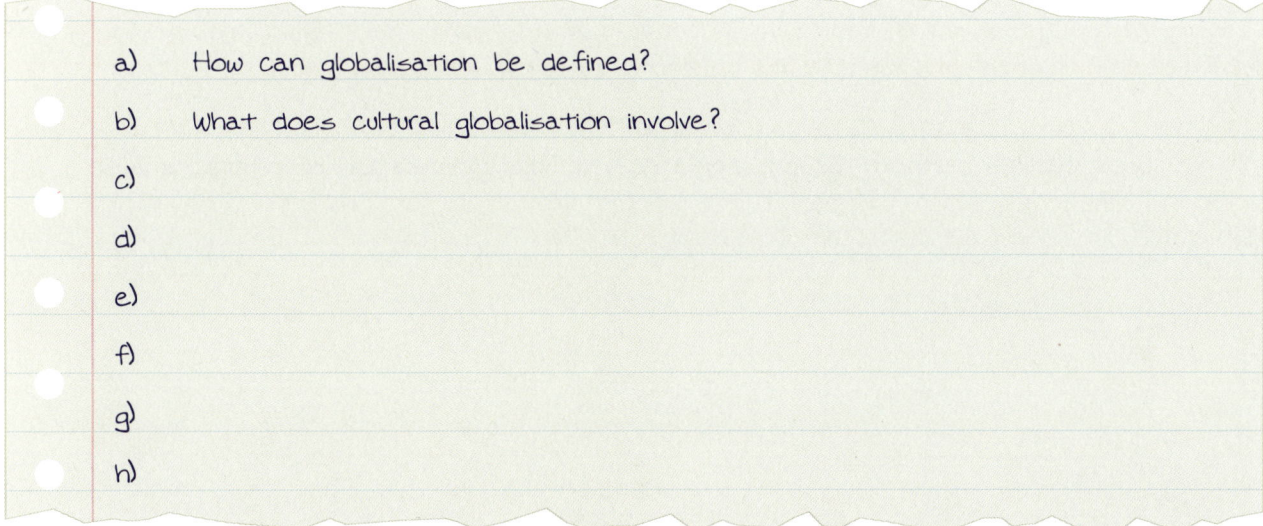

a) How can globalisation be defined?
b) What does cultural globalisation involve?
c)
d)
e)
f)
g)
h)

3.2 Divide up all the research questions between the group. Use the resources available to you to research the questions and take notes. When you are reading, practise applying the criteria given in Unit 1, Task 5 of this module.

3.3 Share the following with the other members of your group:

- the information you have collected;
- your evaluation of the arguments you have read.

Task 4 Developing your argument(s)

You are now going to prepare for the final discussion. It is important to develop your argument(s) so that the discussion helps you to broaden your understanding of the issue, rather than just exchanging opinions. To do this, you need to be clear about your general argument and the more specific arguments which support it.

4.1 To think about your general argument, put a cross on the line below to show where you stand on this issue.

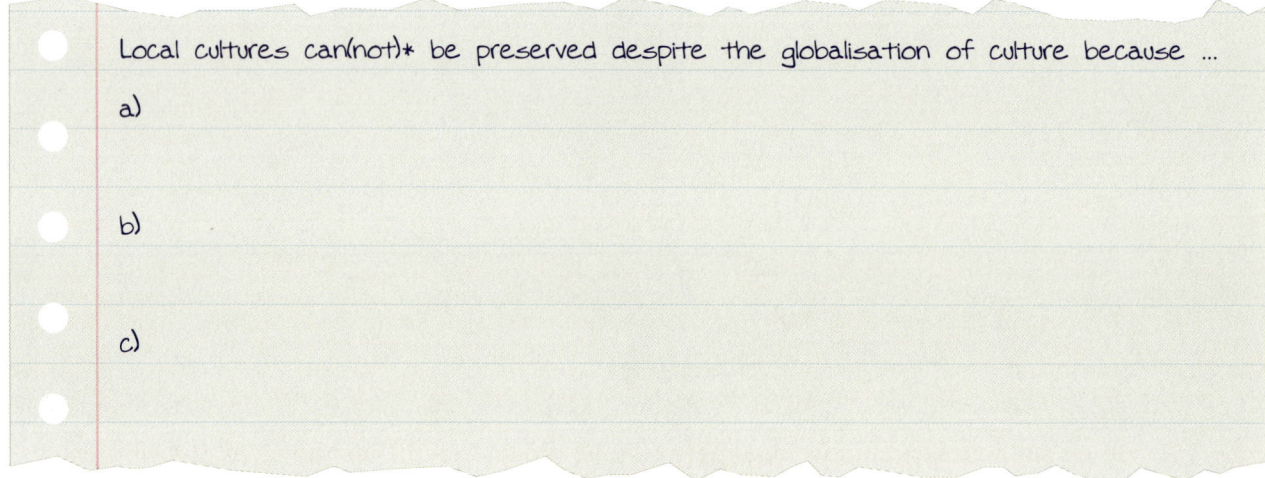

4.2 Now think about why you hold this opinion and write your answers below.

Local cultures can(not)* be preserved despite the globalisation of culture because …

a)

b)

c)

*delete as appropriate

4.3 For each point you wrote in Task 4.2, add a supporting reason. When you have done this, add one or two examples that you have discovered through your group's research.

4.4 Now work with a partner. Explain your overall argument and more specific arguments to each other, and make notes on your partner's ideas.

When you have completed your discussion, evaluate your partner's arguments. Check:

- if the premises support the conclusions in the specific arguments;
- if the specific arguments support the main argument in turn.

Give your partner feedback in a helpful and supportive way.

Task 5 Developing counter-arguments

Predicting how an argument might be countered is a useful exercise. It helps you to strengthen your arguments and prepare a defence of your ideas.

5.1   Take the specific arguments you developed in Tasks 4.2 and 4.3 and predict how another person might counter them.

5.2   Now work with a partner. One of you gives one of your specific arguments with supporting reasons and example(s). The other listens and then gives a counter-argument, with supporting reasons and possibly an example. You then swap roles.

Task 6 The seminar

6.1   Now discuss the question in a seminar group, keeping a note of the arguments put forward by the various speakers.

Task 7 Evaluating the arguments

7.1   Work in a group of three or four students. Use your notes from the seminar to answer the following questions.

   a) Which three arguments you heard in the seminar were most persuasive, and why?

   b) Which three arguments you heard in the seminar were least persuasive, and why?

   c) Did participating in the seminar change your overall opinion?

7.2 **Now work in a new group of three or four students. Discuss the following questions.**

a) Can you think of any examples where speakers used euphemisms or dysphemisms in the seminar? (*Look at Unit 4, Task 1.*)

b) Were there any examples of something being downplayed in the seminar? (*Look at Unit 4, Task 2.*)

c) Were there any examples of overstatement being used? (*Look at Unit 4, Task 3.*)

d) Were there any times in the seminar when you felt a speaker was pressuring you to agree with him or her? (*Look at Unit 4, Task 4.*)

7.3 **Finally, discuss with a partner what you learnt from participating in the seminar.**

Reflect

In this unit, you discussed with other members of your class whether local cultures can be preserved despite globalisation. Imagine various different settings and think about how differently the discussion might have progressed: for example, with your family, with a group of Green activists.

Then think about how this might be influenced if the participants were all of one nationality which had very different cultural values to your own.

Student notes for Unit 6

Module 6

Web work

Website 1 — Critical discussions

http://www.criticalthinking.org/resources/articles/

Review
This website provides an excellent discussion of definitions of critical thinking, articles to read and various other resources.

Task
Go to the ARTICLES link and then on to LEARNING THE ART OF CRITICAL THINKING. Look especially at the *How to* list for dysfunctional living. How many of these statements could apply to you? How can your study of critical thinking help you to change some of those statements?

Website 2 — Critical thinking quiz

http://www.cof.orst.edu/cof/teach/for442/quizzes/q1003.htm

Review
This site takes the form of a fun quiz which should inspire you to think critically. A discussion of the answers is also provided.

Task
Using the quiz as a model, create three questions of your own which also require critical thinking. Try these questions out on a fellow student.

Extension activities

Activity 1

Choose from the resolutions below and conduct in-class debates where different groups take it in turns to support or refute the resolution in question. The audience should vote on which team has carried the resolution.

Resolutions:

a) It is better to work for a small company than a large corporation.
b) Foreign holidays are preferable to holidaying in one's home country.
c) All undergraduate students should be required to live in a hall of residence throughout their time at university.
d) Voting should be compulsory.

When you are planning your arguments, bear in mind the exercises you have completed on what makes a good argument and avoid the pitfalls of poor argumentation.

Activity 2

Find a recent journal in your subject area and critically evaluate one of the articles in the journal, using the checklist from Unit 1.

Activity 3

Listen to an edition of 'Any Questions' on BBC Radio 4 and see if you can note any examples of speakers trying to persuade the audience by using euphemisms or dysphemisms, or by downplaying or overstating a point.

You can listen to an edition of the programme on your radio on Fridays (20.00). Alternatively, you can listen to and find the tapescript of the programme at:

http://www.bbc.co.uk/radio4/news/anyquestions.shtml

Glossary

Analyse (v) To break an issue down into parts in order to study, identify and discuss their meaning and/or relevance.

Bias (n) An attitude you have, or a judgment you have made, based on *subjective opinion* instead of *objective fact*. It can make you treat someone or something in an unfair way.

Common beliefs (n) Ideas that are accepted as true by many people even though there is no evidence for them.

Concept (n) The characteristics or ideas associated with a class or group of objects. For example, the concept 'city' brings to mind traits common to all places classed as 'cities'. 'Paris' is not a concept as it refers to a single, specific place.

Conclusion (n) The final part of a piece of academic writing, talk or presentation which sums up ideas and reaches a final result or judgment.

Counter-argument (n) An argument that opposes or makes the case against another argument.

Critical thinking (n) The academic skill of being able to look at ideas and problems in a considered, critical way in order to *evaluate* them. It also involves the ability to see links between concepts and develop one's own ideas.

Dissuade (v) Make someone stop believing an idea or argument, or prevent them from doing something, by *reasoning* with them.

Downplay (n) Make something seem less important or significant in order to support our own ideas.

Dysphemism (n) An offensive and emotive term or expression that is used to replace a neutral term when we want to make a description sound more negative. For example, 'brat' is a dysphemism for 'child'.

Euphemism (n) A neutral or inoffensive expression that is used to replace a more negative or offensive expression when we want to make something sound more positive. For example, 'pass away' is a euphemism for 'die'.

Evaluate (v) To assess information in terms of quality, relevance, *objectivity* and accuracy.

Fact (n) Something that is known or can be demonstrated to be true.

Fallacy (n) A false belief that is due to faulty reasoning.

Hyperbole (n) Huge overstatement which may be used to *persuade* someone of a *viewpoint*.

Manipulate (v) To influence or control someone else's *opinion* in a dishonest way.

Objective (adj) (n) 1 (adj) Not influenced by personal feelings or emotions. 2 (n) The aim, or what you want to achieve from an activity.

Opinion (n) A personal belief that may be *subjective* and is not based on certainty or *fact*.

Overstate (v) To exaggerate or state in terms that are stronger than necessary.

Paraphrase (v) To alter a piece of text so that you restate it (concisely) in different words without changing its meaning. It is useful to paraphrase when writing a summary of someone's ideas; if the source is acknowledged, it is not plagiarism. It is also possible to paraphrase your own ideas in an essay or presentation; that is, to state them again, often in a clearer, expanded way.

Peer pressure (n) The pressure on someone to conform and look, behave or think in the same way as other people.

Persuade (v) Make someone believe something (such as an idea or argument) or do something, by reasoning with them.

Poor argumentation (n) An argument that is not strong or sound because the *conclusion* does not follow from the *premises*, or because the *premise* is faulty.

Premise (n) A statement that is assumed to be true by an author or speaker who is presenting an argument.

Reasoning (n) The arguments or logic one uses to form *conclusions* and judgments.

Sound argument (n) An argument where the *conclusion* absolutely follows from true *premises*. For example: All cats are carnivores: tigers are cats; therefore, tigers are carnivores. A sound argument is deductive (working from general to particular).

Strategy (n) A plan of action that you follow when you want to achieve a particular goal. For example, it is possible to have a clear strategy for passing an exam.

Strong argument (n) An argument where the *conclusion* does not necessarily follow from the *premises*, but if the *premises* are strong enough the conclusion is likely to be true. For example: Tigers sometimes eat people; therefore, this tiger is likely to eat us. A strong argument is inductive (working from particular to general).

Subjective (adj) Describes an idea or *opinion* that is based on someone's personal opinion rather than on observable phenomena.

Valid argument (n) An argument where the *conclusion* absolutely follows from the *premises*, but the *premises* may not be true. For example: All birds can fly; penguins are birds; therefore, penguins can fly.

Viewpoint (n) The mental position that someone sees things from. For example, the viewpoint of a child is different to that of its parent.

Weak argument (n) An argument which is not *valid*, *strong* or *sound* because the *premises* are wrong and/or the *conclusion* does not follow from the *premises*.

Further notes